SELFIES FROM SPACE

HOW SATELLITES HELP SCIENCE ON EARTH

TAMRA B. ORR

Edge Books are published by Capstone Press,
1710 Roe Crest Drive, North Mankato, Minnesota 56003
www.capstonepub.com

Library of Congress Cataloging-in-Publication Data is available on the Library of Congress website.
ISBN 978-1-5435-7272-8 (library binding)
ISBN 978-1-5435-7517-0 (paperback binding)
ISBN 978-1-5435-7280-3 (eBook PDF)

Editorial Credits
Mandy Robbins, editor; Laura Mitchell, designer; Jo Miller, media researcher;
Katy LaVigne, production specialist

Image Credits
NASA, Cover (Satellite), 24, NASA/Goddard Space Flight Center, 5, 8; Newscom: SIPA/SIPA, 23, UPI/
ESA, 14, ZUMA Press/NASA, 11; NOAA, 16; Science Source: Detlev Van Ravenswaay, 7, Mark Garlick,
29, Planetary Visions Ltd, 13; Shutterstock: AMFPhotography, 21, Christian Wilkinson, 17, robert_s,
Cover (Earth), Vera Petrunina, 19; U.S. Navy photo, 27

Design Elements
Capstone; Shutterstock: Audrius Birbilas

All internet sites appearing in back matter were available and accurate when this book was sent to
press.

Printed and bound in the United States of America.
PA70

TABLE OF CONTENTS

CHAPTER ONE
KEEPING TABS: EYES IN SPACE. 4

CHAPTER TWO
SATELLITES TO THE RESCUE 10

CHAPTER THREE
COMMUNICATION TODAY AND TOMORROW 18

CHAPTER FOUR
SPIES IN THE SKIES. 22

CHAPTER FIVE
KEEPING SATELLITES WORKING 26

GLOSSARY. 30
READ MORE. 31
INTERNET SITES. 31
INDEX. 32

KEEPING TABS: EYES IN SPACE

If you were asked to define the word *satellite*, you might describe a man-made, metal machine moving through space. You would be right. However, those are **artificial** satellites. A satellite is a moon, planet, or machine that **orbits** a planet or star. This means that Earth itself is a satellite because it orbits the Sun. The moon is also a satellite because it orbits Earth.

The first man-made satellites were built in the late 1950s. People sent them into space to learn important information about Earth. More than 60 years later, satellites are still being launched for the same reason. Every day, thousands of artificial satellites circle the planet. They take pictures, send data, and keep track of what is happening on Earth. These eyes in space have changed what we know about the world.

SPACE FACT:

Saturn has many natural satellites with its 62 moons. Between 2004 and 2017, it also had Cassini. This spacecraft spent years orbiting the planet to gather data about Saturn.

artificial—made by people

orbit—to travel around an object in space; an orbit is also the path an object follows while circling an object in space

THE SPACE RACE

The first artificial satellite was called Sputnik. The former Soviet Union launched this space **probe** in October 1957. It was a silver ball, just 23 inches (58 centimeters) across.

The United States rushed to join the Soviets in what was being called "the space race." Both countries wanted to dominate the new territory of outer space. In January 1958, the U.S. sent up its first satellite, the Explorer 1. For years, these two countries focused on launching more complex spacecraft into space. Each satellite brought back more detailed information about Earth's atmosphere, as well as what conditions were like in space. Eventually, this information led to human space flight. The National Aeronautics and Space Administration (NASA) worked to get astronauts on the moon. The Soviets built the first space station. It was called Salyut 1. Astronauts lived there and studied outer space.

As technology developed, more countries launched satellites. These machines could provide amazing amounts of information. They could track the weather and make long-distance phone calls faster. They could even watch Earth's surface for fires or volcanic eruptions. Today thousands of satellites circle Earth.

probe—a small vehicle used to explore objects in outer space

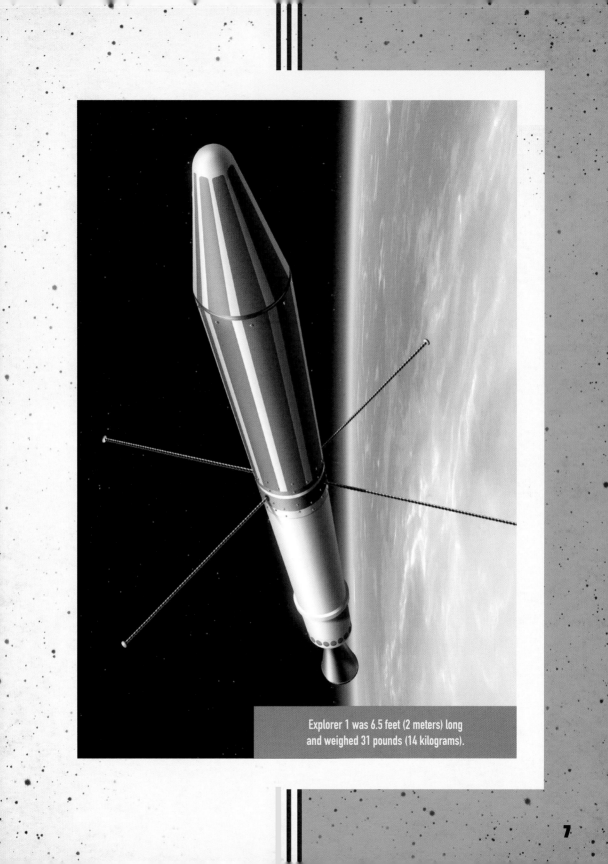

Explorer 1 was 6.5 feet (2 meters) long
and weighed 31 pounds (14 kilograms).

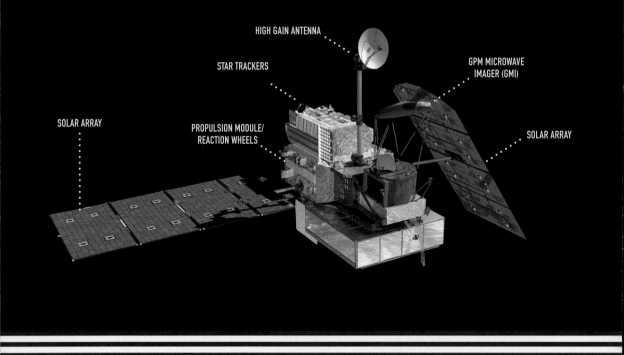

HIGH GAIN ANTENNA

STAR TRACKERS

GPM MICROWAVE IMAGER (GMI)

SOLAR ARRAY

PROPULSION MODULE/ REACTION WHEELS

SOLAR ARRAY

BUILDING AND LAUNCHING SATELLITES

Satellites differ in size and purpose. But they all tend to be made of the same four parts. They have a power system that keeps them running. Most satellites use solar power. Batteries store some of this power to use when the satellite is in darkness. Satellites also all have a way to control their movements and flight. They have equipment to measure or record data such as cameras. Finally, an antenna sends and receives information to and from Earth.

Rockets launch satellites into space. Satellites circle Earth at very high speeds of between 2 and 5 miles (3.2 and 8 kilometers) per second. **Gravity** keeps them in orbit. From Earth, a satellite often looks just like another star. Sunshine reflects off the machine's metal and makes it sparkle in the sky. Unlike stars, however, satellites move.

gravity—a force that pulls objects with mass together; gravity pulls objects down toward the center of Earth

Collision in Space

Space is full of thousands of satellites. Space is so huge that the chance of two objects being in the exact same place at the same time is extremely rare. In 2009, however, a U.S. satellite hit a Russian satellite at 26,000 miles (41,843 km) per hour. Both were destroyed and broke into thousands of pieces. Many of the pieces burned up in Earth's atmosphere. Hundreds more are still floating in space.

CHAPTER TWO

SATELLITES TO THE RESCUE

On August 3, 2018, astronaut Alexander Gerst looked down at Earth from the International Space Station (ISS). He was amazed at what he saw. Below him, he could see that much of California was on fire!

In natural disasters such as California's wildfires, satellites are incredibly helpful. The pictures they take provide images of where fires are raging. They also help experts predict where they will likely spread.

Today satellite images can help first responders in all kinds of emergency situations. First responders and search-and-rescue workers rely on satellites to find people who need help. They use satellite imagery to see what is happening at the scene of disasters. They also use satellites to track where 911 emergency calls are coming from.

Giant plumes of smoke from the 2018 California wildfires were easily viewable from the ISS.

The International Satellite System for Search and Rescue relies on a system of distress emergency beacons linked to satellites. Airplanes or ships can activate these beacons. Hikers can carry these beacons in case they get lost or injured. On average, this agency rescues five people a day.

AN INTERNATIONAL EFFORT

In 2000, the International Charter Space and Major Disasters program was formed to provide satellite technology for first responders. It includes 125 countries and 34 satellites. Space agencies around the world are members. Their satellite data is shared throughout the group. The organization has helped with rescues in earthquakes, floods, fires, volcanic eruptions, and giant ocean waves called tsunamis.

Mapping the Ocean Floor

Today more is known about the geography of the moon and Mars than the ocean floor. But satellites could change that. Currently satellites provide scientists with information about possible tsunamis. As satellite technology improves, humans will have access to even more detailed data. In the future, scientists may be able to use satellites to create detailed maps of each ocean. Spotting shipwrecks, trenches, and underwater volcanoes would be much easier.

This image shows the different types of data that satellites can collect. They include underwater land formations (center), ice cover (bottom left), sea surface temperature (center left), cloud cover (top left), rainfall levels (top right), plant life (center right), and wind speed (bottom right).

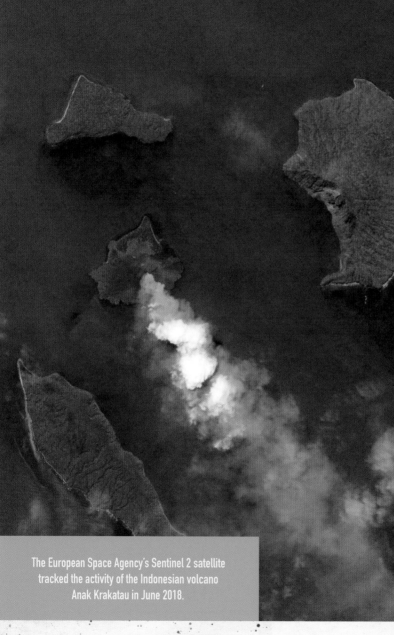

The European Space Agency's Sentinel 2 satellite
tracked the activity of the Indonesian volcano
Anak Krakatau in June 2018.

TRACKING POSSIBLE RISKS

Satellites don't just help during disasters. They can also help people prepare for them. Currently, satellites use data about rainfall to pinpoint areas most at risk for floods or landslides. By tracking a hurricane, satellites can help first responders and disaster teams determine where the storm might make landfall. This is where the storm would be most threatening to people's safety.

Detailed pictures of Earth's surface can provide important clues about possible earthquakes. They can also let people know if an erupting volcano is going to send lava their way. Satellites can even track the **ash plume** that comes from these volcanoes. The ash is dangerous to jet engines, so planes need to know where it is safe to fly. As satellites improve, scientists hope to see patterns develop so they can predict an eruption before it happens.

By getting this information from satellites, first responders and governments can better respond to disasters. The data also helps people know if they have to **evacuate**. This can give them the time they need to gather the most important supplies before trouble appears.

ash plume—the cloud of smoke, ash, and gases that follows a volcanic eruption
evacuate—to move to safety quickly

The GOES East satellite tracked Hurricane Florence as it was about to make landfall along the United States East Coast on September 13, 2018.

SPACE FACT:

Satellites track temperatures and rainfall. Scientists use this information to predict where mosquitos will breed. Mosquitoes can carry disease. Knowing their location helps experts know where to send medical help.

NASA'S EARTH SCIENCE DISASTERS PROGRAM

In 2008, NASA's Earth Science Disasters Program combined satellite data with communities in need of help. It works with local, national, and international disaster response agencies to help them battle the biggest natural disasters. In 2010, it helped track the movement of oil after the Deepwater Horizon spill in the Gulf of Mexico. Five years later, it provided maps of the most damaged areas following Nepal's Gorkha earthquake. In 2018, the disasters team helped with power outages from Hurricane Michael in Florida. They also helped during flooding from Hurricane Florence in North Carolina and threats from the wildfires in California. In the future, NASA hopes it will be able to send up even better satellites.

Penguins and Poo Patterns

Climate change poses a serious risk to life on Earth. Scientists can monitor the changes by tracking melting of polar ice. They do this by tracking Adélie penguins in Antarctica. They look for their bright pink poop, or guano. These "poo views" indicate how many penguins are in each area. Monitoring the penguin population reflects the overall health of the environment. A dropping number of penguins often means trouble, such as melting polar ice.

CHAPTER THREE

COMMUNICATION TODAY AND TOMORROW

Imagine if all of the satellites suddenly stopped working. Life would be incredibly different—and a lot less convenient. You might not be able to watch much television. Satellites send television signals into many homes. If you do get TV, live reporting from reporters on the scene would stop since those last-minute reports are sent via satellite.

Communication would also be far more difficult without satellites. International calls would be almost impossible. Internet connections would either slow down dramatically or fail. Most cell phones would be useless. Using GPS to get directions would be impossible. Almost all banking would come to a grinding halt. Current weather reports would not be available either.

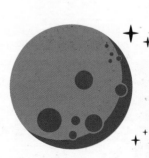

SPACE FACT:

In 2018, almost 25 million people in the United States relied on GPS in their vehicles for directions. Experts predict that number will reach 27 million in 2020.

TRACKING WEATHER PATTERNS

Currently weather satellites help scientists predict daily and weekly upcoming weather patterns. They are hoping that one day they will have satellites that will be able to predict several months of weather at a time.

Some companies are even researching using satellites to control the weather! Having this power could mean stopping the rain in flooded areas or sending rain to areas hit by drought. It could weaken the power of a tornado, hurricane, or tropical storm. This could protect people, crops, and livestock.

A Real Challenge

For high school students around the world, MIT offers the SPHERES Zero Robotics challenge. Teams of students write mathematical formulas to instruct robotic satellites to do a specific task. In the past, teams wrote the code for the completion of a solar power station. Their formulas directed a satellite to join, or dock, with a floating solar panel. The best designs are chosen to send to the satellites on the ISS.

Researchers have considered everything from "seeding clouds" with **silver iodide** to sending laser pulses into clouds to get rid of raindrops. Finding the best way to control the weather is challenging. Researchers are still trying to figure out how to get this technology to the satellites. They're also working on how to install it and how to get the satellites to put it into action.

SPACE FACT:

The Cyclone Global Navigation Satellite System measures a hurricane's wind speeds. This information helps weather forecasters make better predictions about the hurricane's strength and path.

silver iodide—a compound that has the ability to freeze certain types of water

CHAPTER FOUR

SPIES IN THE SKIES

Many satellites work to protect people from disasters. Others are used to keep people connected to each other. But other types of satellites are known as "spy satellites." They are mainly used to protect nations from threats.

Keyhole-class (KH) satellites have been circling the planet for more than 30 years. They are basically giant cameras with huge lenses. Their main job is to take pictures of military missions around the world. Their locations in the sky are kept secret at all times. Militaries use the information to know the location of forces that could be a threat. They also use the data to map certain areas and give this information to troops on the ground.

OSAMA BIN LADEN'S RESIDENCE

A U.S. spy satellite helped military officials locate terrorist Osama bin Laden's compound. Navy SEALs were then able to plan their attack in 2011.

Satellites play a big part in **intelligence**, navigation, communications, and warfare. Military satellites can see in the dark. They can monitor the oceans for ships and submarines. They can keep track of weapons and **nuclear** abilities. The U.S. government is looking at ways to increase how quickly their satellites can transfer data. They also want to keep signals from getting jammed by outside technology.

SPACE FACT:

The United States has more than 120 military satellites. Russia and China each have about 70. These numbers change every year.

intelligence—secret information
nuclear—having to do with the energy created by splitting atoms

The NanoRacks Launcher on the Japanese robotic arm of the ISS releases a set of cube-shaped satellites, or CubeSats.

SPACE FACT:

Canada's CubeSat is a program made up of student teams dedicated to developing tiny satellites. Winning designs will be launched off the ISS in 2020 and 2021.

THE FUTURE OF
SATELLITE TECHNOLOGY

The abilities of satellites are growing.
But their actual size is shrinking. Cube-shaped
satellites, similar in size to a Rubik's cube, are
still big enough to hold sensors and other
high-tech instruments. A number of companies
are producing these small machines, including
Spain's Aistech and joint European and American
company GomSpace. Both believe that smaller
satellites mean lower costs and less concern of
collision when a satellite wears out.

Satellites could one day be built in space,
rather than on Earth. They would then be sent
farther into space attached to a rocket. Making
satellites tough enough to cope with the shock
and pressure of launching means adding pounds
of support structures that are not needed once the
satellite is in space. The American-based Made in
Space company is working with NASA to build an
Archinaut. According to NASA, the Archinaut is a
"mini-fridge-sized" robot. It will be installed on
the ISS. Its robotic arm is designed to do simple
construction in space. It is the first step to putting
together satellites in space.

CHAPTER FIVE

KEEPING SATELLITES WORKING

Satellites are amazing, but they don't last forever. Sometimes they have a glitch. Sometimes they need repairs. Sometimes they have a problem with their energy supply. Repairing or refueling a machine in space presents a huge challenge.

Satellites that cannot be fixed are sometimes sent into "graveyard orbit" by mission control. To do this, engineers force the satellite to fire its engines until it reaches a distant orbit. There it will be out of the way of other spacecraft.

Controllers can also shoot down damaged satellites if there is a danger of them falling to Earth. Sometimes these "shootdowns" go well, and sometimes they don't. In 2007, China shot down an old weather satellite. The resulting explosion created a huge cloud of debris. The broken pieces posed a serious risk to other satellites and spacecraft. At orbital speeds, even tiny collisions are dangerous.

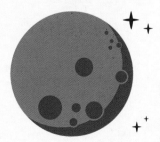

A U.S. missile shoots into space to destroy decaying satellite USA 193.

SPACE FACT:

In February 2008, satellite USA 193 was hurtling toward Earth with a tank full of toxic fuel. A military missile blasted it to pieces before it reached the planet.

SPACE ROBOTS

Repairing satellites in space can be challenging. Today organizations such as the U.S. Defense Advanced Research Projects Agency (DARPA) are working to build machines with very complex, flexible arms. These robots will be able to repair, refuel, and service the world's satellites.

Future satellites will likely have parts that can be swapped in and out like today's computers. Parts will be plugged in until they malfunction. Then they will simply be replaced. This will keep the satellites working longer without the huge cost of replacing the entire structure.

The satellites the world has today would have seemed impossible only 30 or 40 years ago. They supply the world with so much important information. It is hard to imagine life without them. What they will be like tomorrow is still a mystery, but it is sure to be incredible.

SPACE FACT:
In April 2018, NASA launched the Transiting Exoplanet Survey Satellite. It is known as TESS. TESS's job for the next two years will be looking for worlds that could support life.

Scientists expect TESS to find about 20,000 new planets.

GLOSSARY

artificial (ar-tuh-FISH-uhl)—made by people

ash plume (ASH PLOOM)—the cloud of smoke, ash, and gases that follows a volcanic eruption

evacuate (i-VAH-kyoo-wayt)—to move to safety quickly

gravity (GRAV-uh-tee)—a force that pulls objects with mass together; gravity pulls objects down toward the center of Earth

guano (GWAH-no)—droppings of waste from an animal

hurricane (HER-uh-kayn)—a severe tropical storm

intelligence (in-TEL-uh-jinss)—secret information

nuclear (NOO-klee-ur)—having to do with the energy created by splitting atoms

orbit (OR-buht)—to travel around an object in space; an orbit is also the path an object follows while circling an object in space

probe (PROHB)—a small vehicle used to explore objects in outer space

silver iodide (SIL-vuhr EYE-uh-dide)—compound that has the ability to freeze certain types of water

tsunamis (su-NAH-mee)—a series of large, destructive ocean waves, commonly caused by an earthquake

READ MORE

Baker, David and Heather *Kissock. Satellites.* All about Space Science. New York: AV2 by Weigl, 2017.

Graham, Ian. *You Wouldn't Want to Live without Satellites!* You Wouldn't Want to Live Without. New York: Franklin Watts, an Imprint of Scholastic Inc., 2019.

Hamilton, John. *The Space Race.* Missiles and Spy Satellites. Minneapolis: Abdo Pub., 2019.

Woolf, Alex. *The Science of Spacecraft: The Cosmic Truth about Rockets, Satellites, and Probes.* The Science of . . .. New York: Franklin Watts, an imprint of Scholastic Inc., 2019.

INTERNET SITES

Satellites
www.esa.int/kids/en/learn/Technology/Useful_space/Satellites

Space Facts
www.sciencekids.co.nz/sciencefacts/space/satellites.html

What is a Satellite?
www.nasa.gov/audience/forstudents/5-8/features/nasa-knows/
what-is-a-satellite-58.html

Adélie penguins, 17

cameras, 8, 22
Cassini, 5
climate change, 17
CubeSats, 24, 25
Cyclone Global Navigation Satellite
    System, 21

earthquakes, 12, 15, 17
Earth Science Disasters Program, 17
Explorer 1, 6

fires, 6, 10, 12, 17

Gerst, Alexander, 10

International Charter Space and Major
    Disasters, 12
International Satellite System for
    Search and Rescue, 11
International Space Station (ISS), 10,
    20, 24, 25

keyhole-class (KH) satellites, 22–23

moon, 4, 6, 12

National Aeronautics and Space
    Administration (NASA), 6, 17, 25, 28

oceans, 12

Salyut 1, 6
satellite repairs, 26, 28
Saturn, 5
space race, the, 6
SPHERES Zero Robotics challenge, 20
Sputnik, 6

Transiting Exoplanet Survey Satellite
    (TESS), 28

U.S. Defense Advanced Research
    Projects Agency (DARPA), 28

volcanoes, 6, 12, 15

weather, 6, 18, 20–21, 26
    hurricanes, 15, 17, 20, 21
    storms, 15, 20